INTERESTING FACTS ABOUT JAGUAR

facts with Picture book

Jaguars are the largest cats in the Americas and the third largest cats in the world, after lions and tigers.

They have a distinctive rosette pattern on their fur, which helps them blend in with their surroundings in the dense rainforests where they live.

Jaguars are excellent swimmers and are known to catch fish and even swim across rivers to hunt for prey.

They are solitary animals and only come together to mate.

Jaguars have been known to take down prey as large as caimans, peccaries, monkeys, and deer.

The jaguar is an apex predator and plays an important role in controlling the populations of prey species in its ecosystem.

They are considered a near threatened species due to habitat loss and hunting.

How long are they?

The length of a jaguar is 1.1 to 1.8 meters.

What is their height?

The height of a jaguar is 63 to 76 cm.

Jaguars are powerful animals. They look like leopards but differ in many ways.

Are they nocturnal or diurnal?

They are both nocturnal and diurnal

How much do they weigh?

Their weight varies from 56 to 96 kg.

What is the color of their eyes?

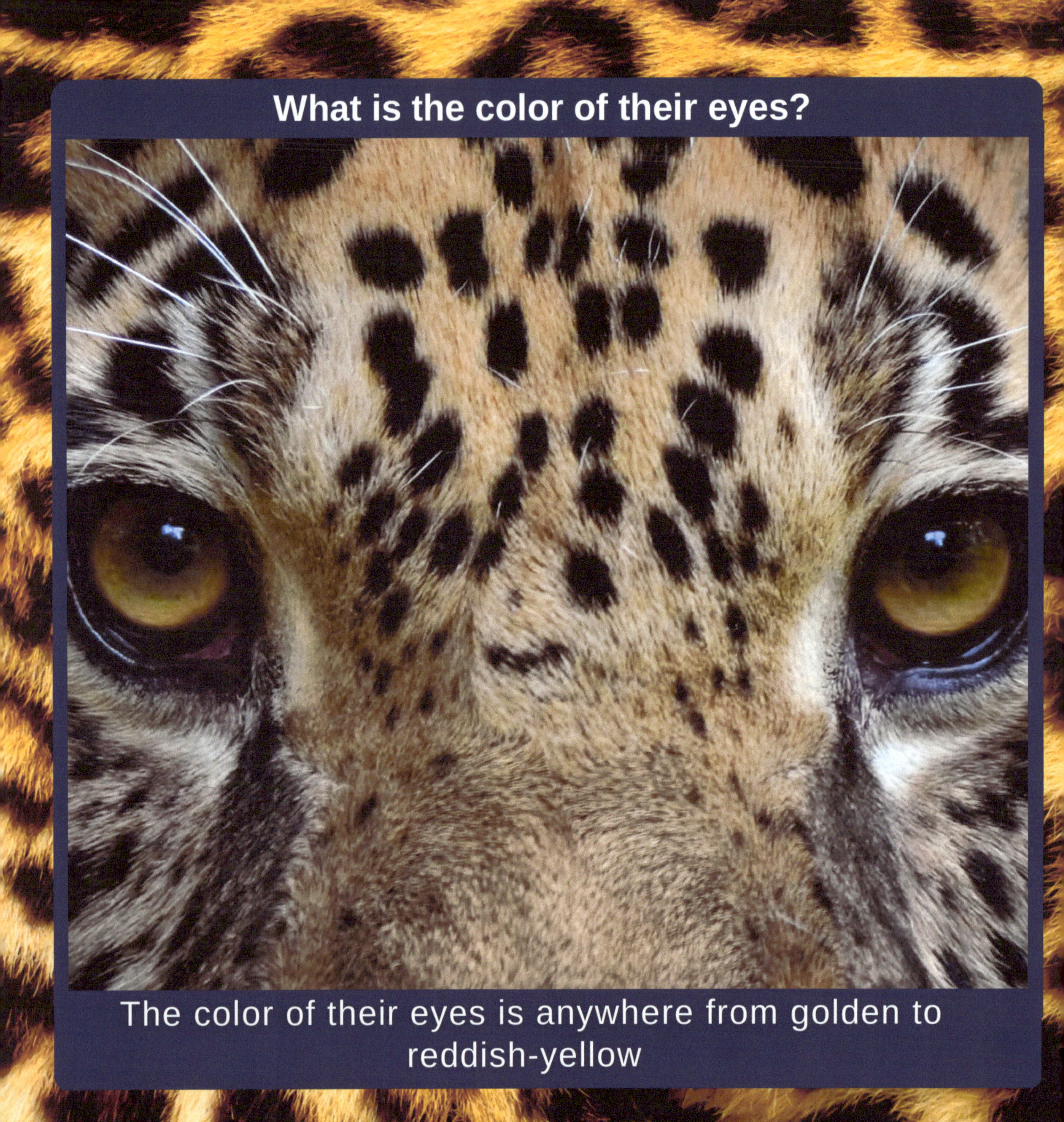

The color of their eyes is anywhere from golden to reddish-yellow

How long can their tails grow?

Their tails can grow to over 80 cm.

How long do they live for?

They live for about 12 to 15 years.

What is a group or family of jaguar called?

A group or family of a jaguar is called 'leap' or 'prowl'.

How long do jaguars sleep for?

Jaguars sleep for over 10 hours every day.

Where do they sleep?

Jaguars sleep on a tree, hugging its branch.

What do jaguars do at night?

Jaguars travel up to 60 miles every night to hunt their prey.

How strong is their bite?

Among all the big cats, jaguars are known to have the strongest bite.

Do jaguars bite?

Yes, the bite of a jaguar is very powerful.

Can they see well?

Jaguars cannot see very well during the daytime but their vision is excellent during the night.

Do they roar?

Yes, jaguars roar.

What is their call called?

A jaguar's call is called a 'saw'.

What is a baby jaguar called?

A baby jaguar is called a 'cub'.

Can baby jaguars see?

No, their eyes are closed when they are born. Cubs can see after they are 6 months old.

How many cubs can a female jaguar birth at a time?

A female jaguar can birth up to 4 cubs at a time.

For how many days does a female carry its cub?

A female jaguar carries its cub inside her for 100 days.

How long does the cub live with its mother?

The jaguar's baby lives with its mother for about 1.5 years.

What color eyes does a cub have?

A baby jaguar has blue eyes.

Who are the predators of jaguars?

Jaguars are largely hunted by humans; they have no natural predators.

What are the prey of jaguars?

Jaguars eat many mammals, reptiles, and birds.

Where do they eat their prey?

Jaguars tend to drag their prey into the trees and then munch on it.

How do jaguars catch fish?

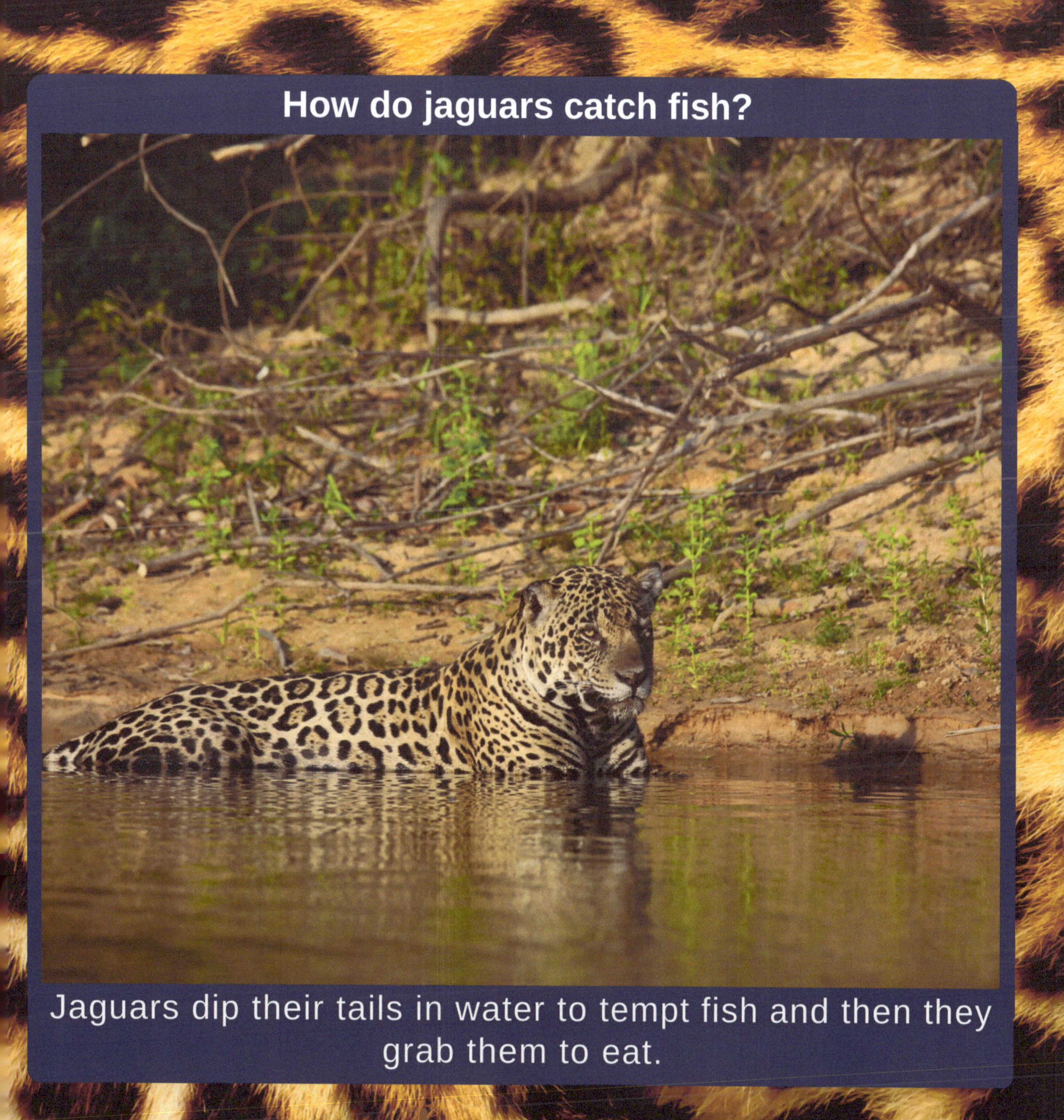

Jaguars dip their tails in water to tempt fish and then they grab them to eat.

Where are they found?

They are largely found in the Pantanal and Amazon Rain forest.

How many jaguars are left in the world?

There are about 173,000 jaguars left in the world.

Are they friendly?
Jaguars don't attack humans a lot unless they feel threatened.

How fast can jaguars run?

Jaguars can run at a speed of 80 kilometers per hour.

Can they be pets?

No, keeping them as pets is very dangerous.

Do they like water?

Yes, jaguars love to spend their time in the water.

Can jaguars swim?

Yes, jaguars are very good swimmers!